W9-AAZ-276

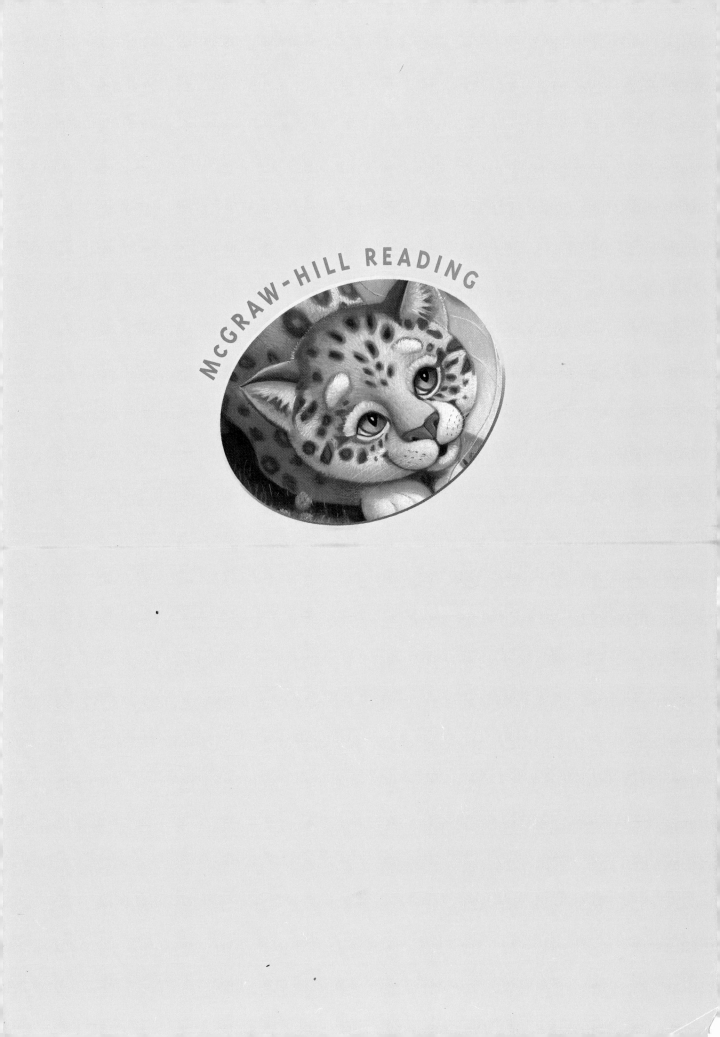

McGRAW-HILL READING

Consulting Authors

Barbara Coulter, Frankie Dungan, Joseph B. Rubin,
Carl B. Smith, Shirley Wright

Contributors

The Princeton Review, Time Magazine

The Princeton Review is not
affiliated with Princeton
University or ETS.

McGraw-Hill School Division

A Division of The McGraw·Hill Companies

McGraw-Hill School Division
Two Penn Plaza
New York, New York 10121

Printed in the United States of America

ISBN 0-02-184729-0/1, Book 1
    4 5 6 7 8 9 043/071 04 03 02 01 00

Macmillan/McGraw-Hill Edition

McGRAW-HILL READING

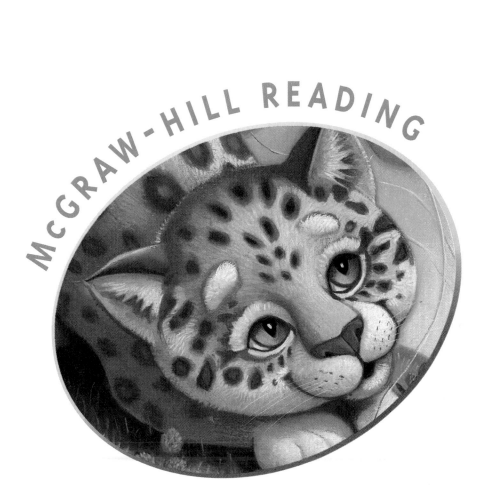

Authors

James Flood
Jan E. Hasbrouck
James V. Hoffman
Diane Lapp
Angela Shelf Medearis
Scott Paris
Steven Stahl
Josefina Villamil Tinajero
Karen D. Wood

**McGraw-Hill
School Division**

New York   Farmington

Day by Day

Day by Day

The Tickle Rhyme

"Who's that tickling my back?"
said the wall.
"Me," said a small
Caterpillar. "I'm learning
To crawl."

by Ian Serraillier

Nap, Cat

Nap with a bat, cat?

Nap with a mat, cat?

Nap with a map, cat?

Nap with a cap, cat?

The best place to nap, cat,

Is to nap on my lap!

Meet Ann Morris

Ann Morris has taught in many public and private schools. She has also made several award-winning films for children. Now she spends most of her time writing children's books.

Meet Kathi Ember

Kathi Ember has two horses, three sheep, and four cats. Her pets give her ideas for her illustrations. She has illustrated children's books, greeting cards, and magazines.

Max, the Cat

by Ann Morris

illustrated by
Kathi Ember

Pam has a cat.

He is Max.

Pam has a mat.

Max likes to nap on the mat.

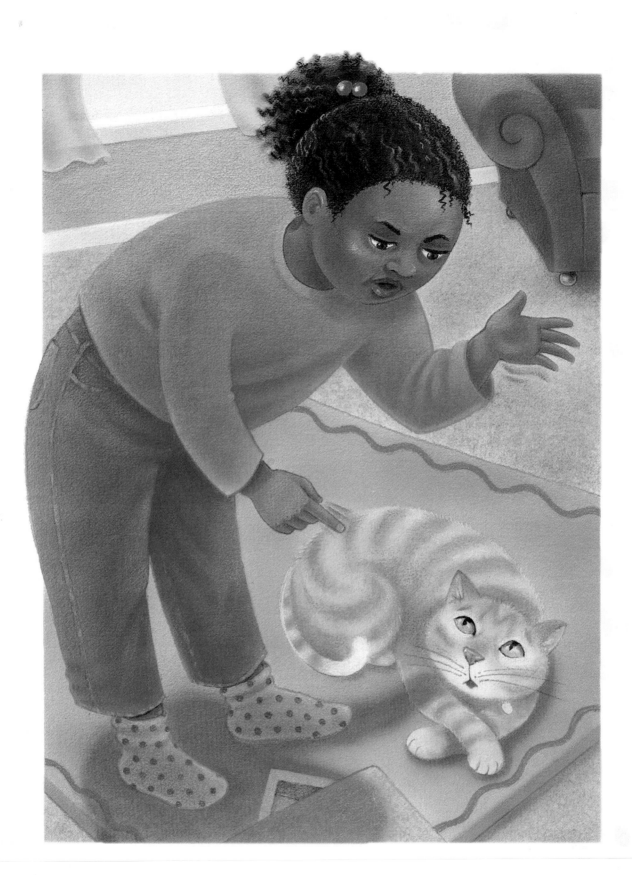

Max can not nap on this mat.

Pam has a cap.

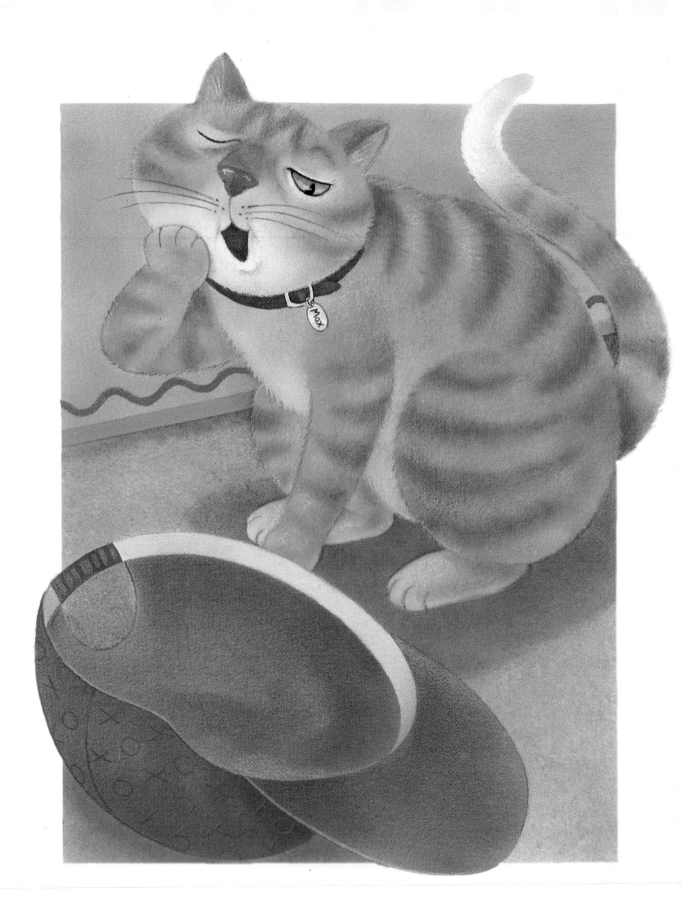

Max likes to nap in this cap.

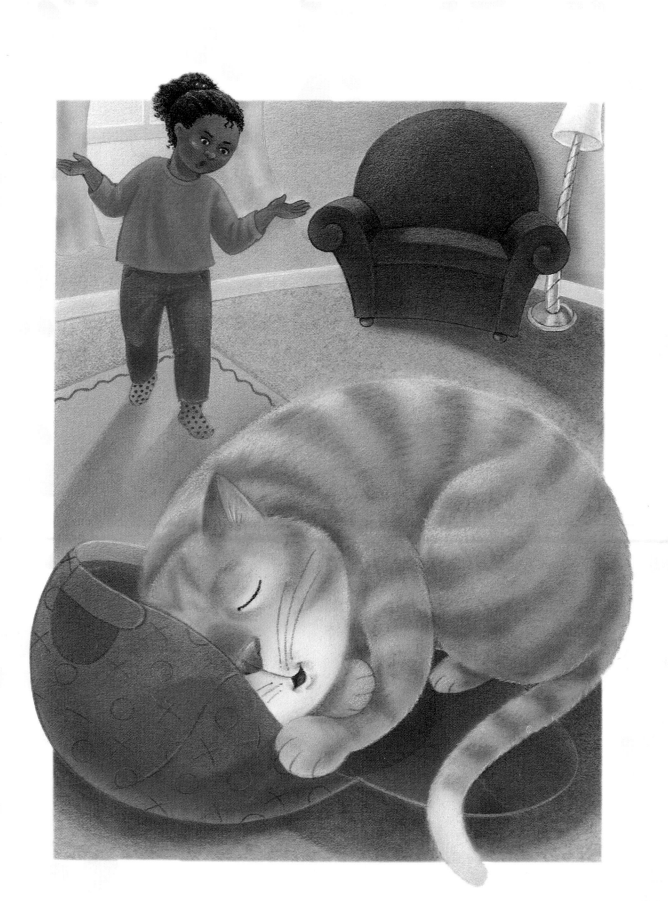

Max can not nap in this cap.

Pam is mad.

Max is mad.

Pam is sad.

Max is sad.

Pam gives Max one hug.

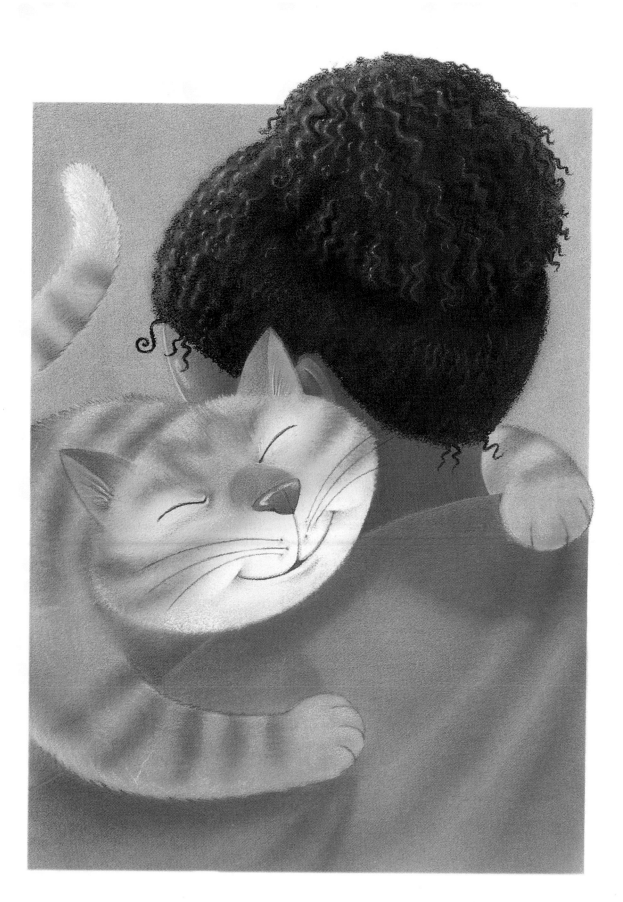

Max gives Pam one hug.

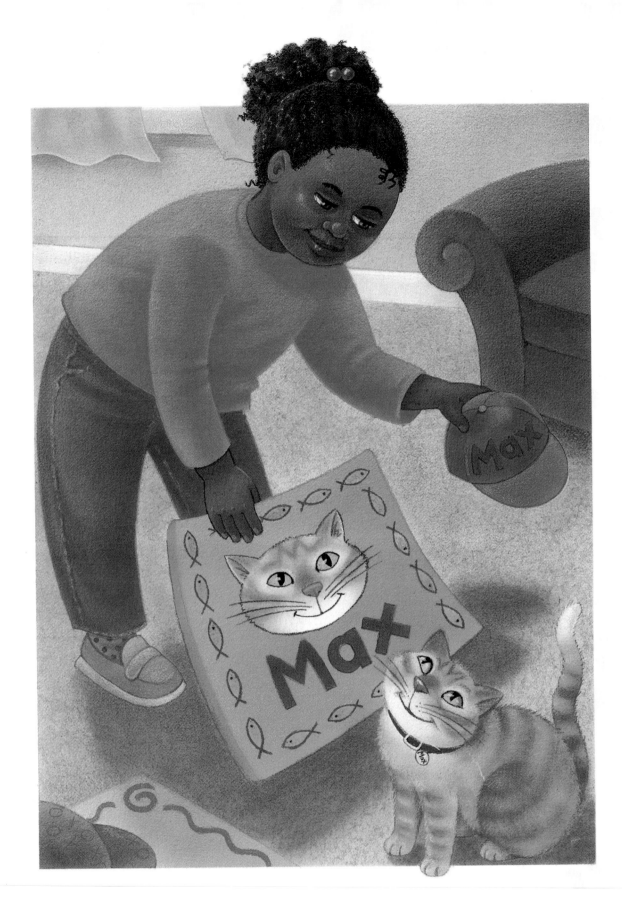

Pam gives Max a mat and a cap.

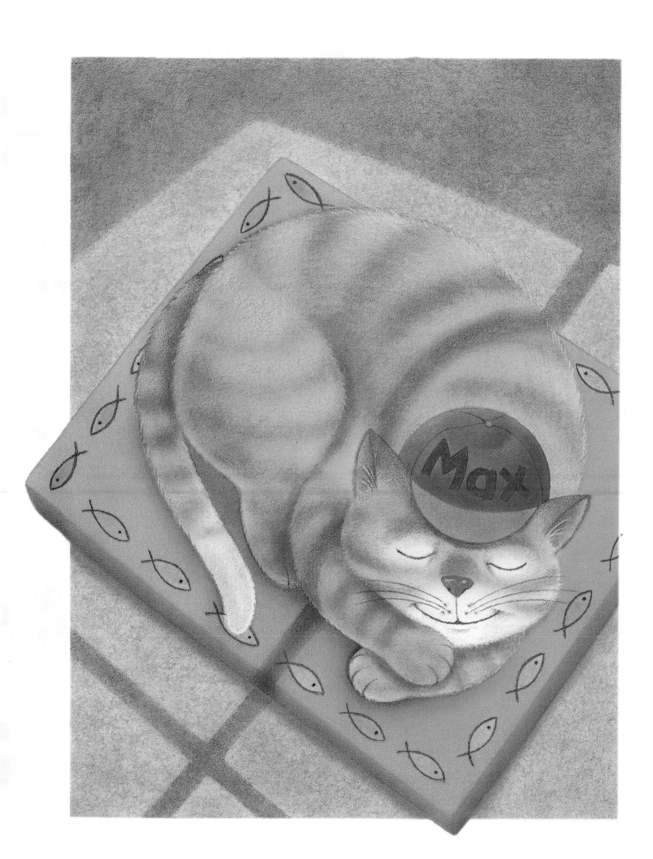

Now Max naps and naps.

Story Questions & Activities

1 What does Pam have?

2 Why is Pam mad?

3 What else might Max like?

4 What is "Max, the Cat" about?

5 Is Max like a cat you read about?

Name a Cat

Draw a mat for a cat.
Write the name of the
cat on the mat.

Sam

Make a Cat

Cut shapes out of paper.
Make a cat with the shapes.
Glue the cat on paper.

Find Out More

Some cats are good pets.
Some cats are wild.
Find out about a wild cat.

29

Parts of a Book

Cover

title

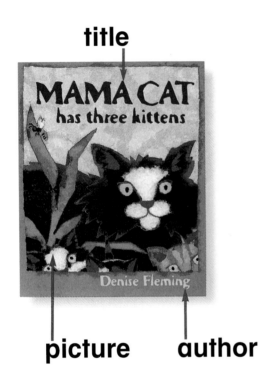

picture   author

Title Page

title

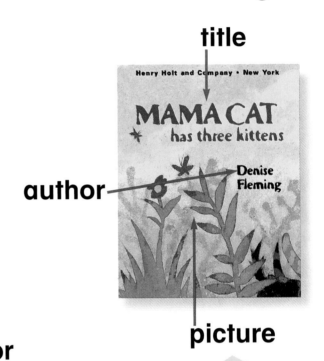

author

picture

Look at the Parts of a Book

1 What is on the book cover?

2 What is on the title page?

30

Cat Wakes Up

Cat wakes up.

She wants food.

She will cry.

Let us feed her.

Now, she is a happy cat.

What is the title of this story?

○ The Happy Cat

○ Cat Wakes Up

The title can tell you about the story.

The Sack

Quack! Quack! Quack! Quack!

I pack a tan sack.

I pack my hat.

And I pack my bat.

I pack my ball,

And give it all to Jack.

Meet Judi Barrett

Judi Barrett has always enjoyed creating things. When she was a child, she enjoyed writing and illustrating stories. Today, she still enjoys creating the words and pictures for many children's books.

Meet Luisa D'Augusta

When Luisa D'Augusta was little, she drew many funny pictures. Today, she illustrates many children's books.

34

Quack

by Judi Barrett

illustrated by Luisa D'Augusta

This is Dad.

That is the van.

Jack and Mack help Dad.

They pack the van.

I help pack.

I pack my bat.

I pack my hat.

I pack my map.

43

I pack my cap on my bat.

Jack hears a quack quack.

"What is that quack?" says Jack.

"Do not pack your Quack in back!"

49

Dad packs me and Quack.

Good-bye, Jack and Mack!

1 Who helps Dad pack?

2 Why didn't Mack and Jack get in the van?

3 Why are Dad and Nan moving?

4 Tell what Nan packed.

5 How is Quack like Max the Cat?

Make a List

Pretend you are moving.
List what you would pack.

Make a Van

Fold a paper in half.

Draw a van on one side.

Cut the van out.

Do not cut on the fold.

Stand it up.

Find Out More

There are many kinds of ducks.

Find pictures of them.

Tell how they are alike and different.

STUDY SKILLS

Parts of a Book

author

illustrator

Hattie and the Fox
by Mem Fox
Illustrated by Patricia Mullins

An author writes a story.

An illustrator draws the pictures.

Sometimes the author is also the illustrator.

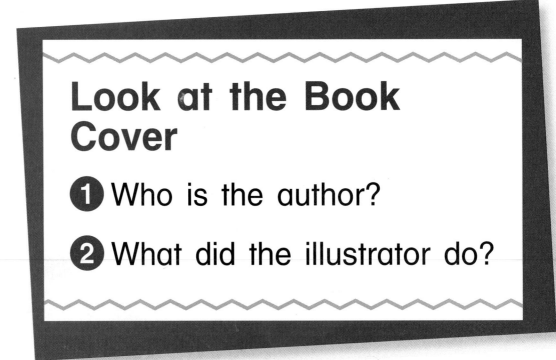

Look at the Book Cover

1 Who is the author?

2 What did the illustrator do?

On the Pond

There is a duck on the pond.

There is a frog on the pond.

The duck quacks at the frog.

The frog croaks at the duck.

The duck swims after the frog.

The frog swims away.

What is on the pond?

○ A duck

○ A swan

Sometimes pictures give clues about the story.

Jig and Tap

I see a pig in a wig.

The pig in the wig

Can dance a quick jig!

I see a pig in a cap.

The pig in the cap

Can tap and tap!

Meet Angela Shelf Medearis

Angela Shelf Medearis has loved reading books since she was a child. There were few books by or about African Americans then. Now that she is grown up, Medearis enjoys writing about African Americans.

Meet Barbara Reid

Barbara Reid has always liked to tell stories with pictures. After going to art school, she became a children's book illustrator. Many of her books have won awards.

what Does Pig Do?

by Angela Shelf Medearis

illustrated by Barbara Reid

On Monday, Pig picks a wig.

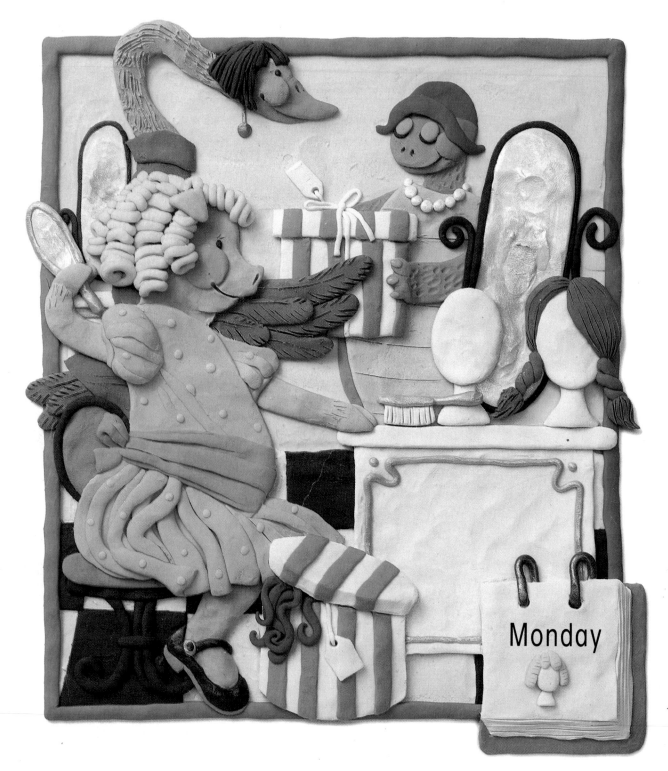

Monday

On Tuesday, Pig digs and digs.

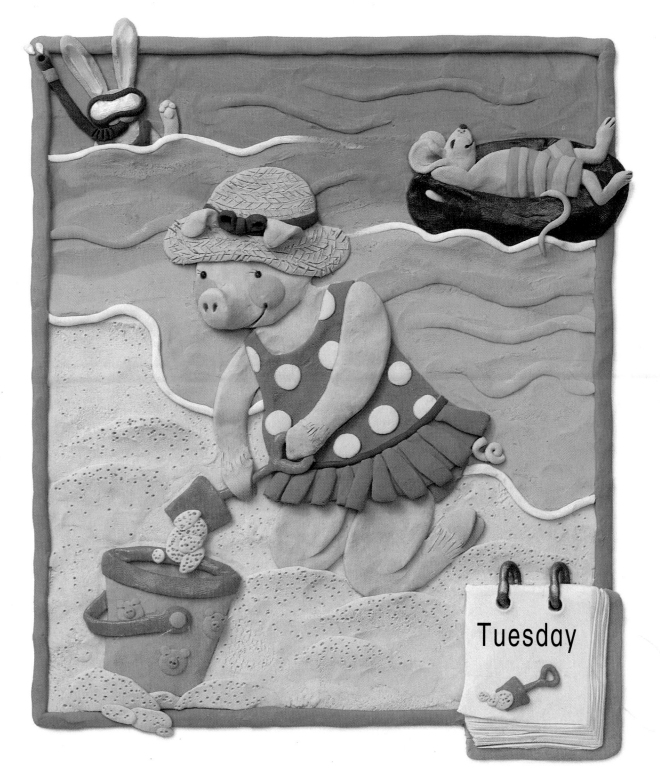

Tuesday

On Wednesday, Pig kicks and kicks.

Wednesday

On Thursday, Pig taps and taps.

On Friday, Pig bats.

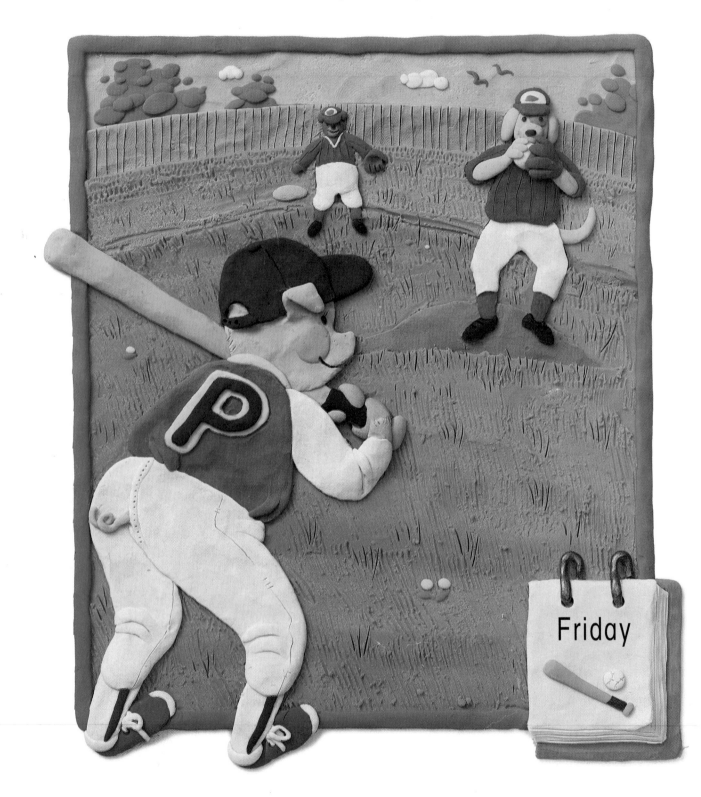

On Saturday, Pig does laps.

What does Pig do on Sunday?

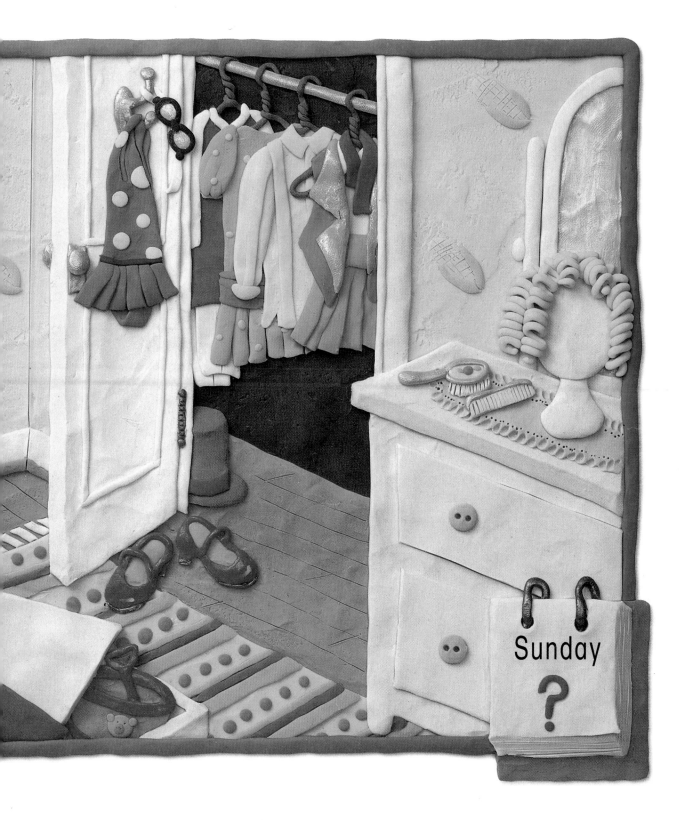

Sunday

?

Pig does not pick a wig.

Pig does not dig and dig.

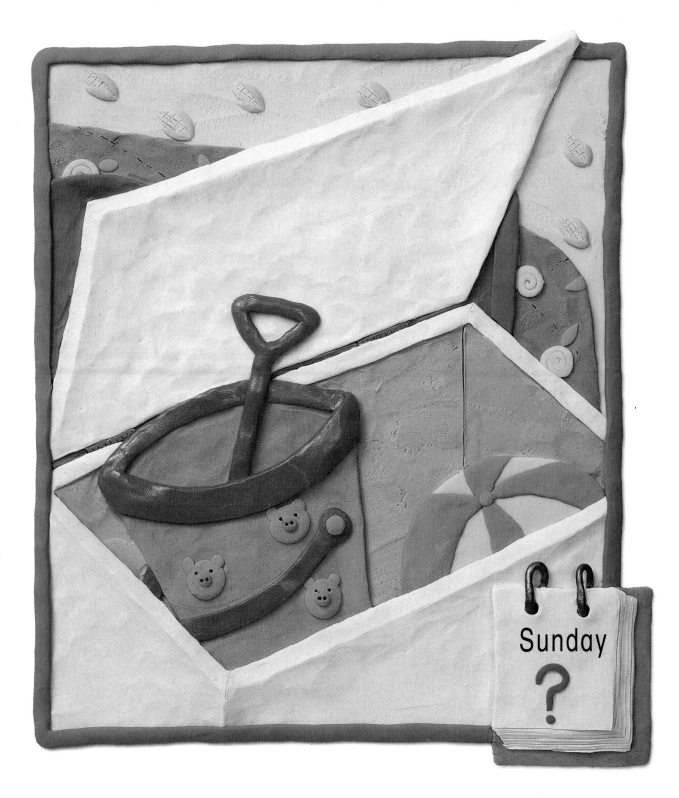

Pig does not kick and kick.

Pig does not tap and tap.

Sunday
?

Pig does not bat.

Sunday

?

Pig does not do laps.

What does Pig do on Sunday?

There is Pig!

Look at her!

On Sunday, Pig naps!

1 What does Pig do on Friday?

2 What does Pig's calendar show?

3 Why is it good to have a calendar?

4 Act out the story.

5 In what ways are Pig and Max, the Cat the same?

Make a Calendar

Pick a day of the week.
Draw a box.
Write the day at the top.
Draw what you do on
that day.

Thursday

Friday

Make a Class Book

A shovel and a pail go together.

So do a bat and a ball.

Draw two things that go together.

Make a class book.

THIS IS BASEBALL

by Margaret Blackstone
pictures by John O'Brien

Find Out More

Choose a game or sport.

Find out how to play it.

STUDY SKILLS

Parts of a Book

A table of contents tells what is in a book.

It tells the page where each story begins.

Look at the Table of Contents

1 What story begins on page 19?

2 Where does "The Guest" begin?

Where Was the Pig?

Pam had a pig.

It hid in the tub.

Then, it hid in the car.

Then, it hid in the bed.

Pam found her pig.

It was asleep.

Where did the pig hide first?

○ In the tub

○ In the bed

Read the story carefully.

Fish Dish

"I wish, wish, wish
For a dish," said the fish,
"With a yam, yam, yam,
And a little bit of jam,
And I want thin ham
With that yam!" said the fish.

Meet Jean Marzollo

Jean Marzollo likes to write children's books. She says, "It's a job, a hobby, and a game—all in one." Marzollo also likes to visit schools and talk to children about her work.

Meet Peggy Tagel

Peggy Tagel has drawn illustrations for magazines, greeting cards, and children's books. She also likes to garden and collect cookie jars.

84

THE PATH ON THE MAP

by Jean Marzollo

illustrated by Peggy Tagel

We have a map.

The map has a path.

Let's go down this path.

Let's see what is on this map.

A pig is on this map.

Can you see it?

A fat cow is on this map.

Can you see it?

A duck is on this map.

Can you see it?

95

A fish is on this map.

That is a big fish!

A tan cat is on the path.

Can you see it on the map?

A shack is on this map.

What could be in the shack?

Let's look.

102

More cats!

1 What animals are in the pond?

2 How did the map help the children?

3 What else might be in the shack?

4 Use the map to retell the story.

5 What other story has a map?

Write About a Picture

Choose one farm animal.
Write two sentences about it.

Make an Animal

Choose a farm animal.

Make the animal with clay.

Find Out More

Look at a map of the United States.

Find your state.

Find your city.

Glossary

A Glossary is at the end of this book.

Each word in it has a picture.

The words are in ABC order.

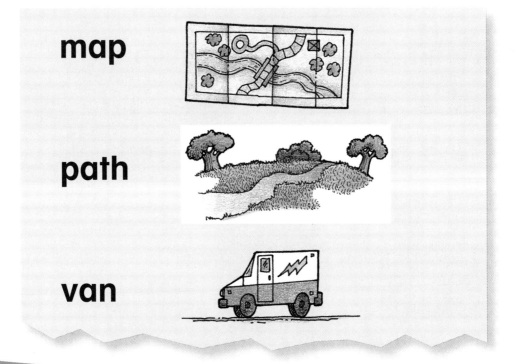

map

path

van

Look at the Glossary

1 What word comes after *map*?

2 What word shows a kind of car?

Who Went to the Farm?

First, the hen went to the farm.

Then, the cow went to the farm.

Next, the lamb went to the farm.

Last, the boy went to the farm.

Then, the farm was full.

Who went to the farm last?

○ The lamb

○ The boy

Read the question carefully before you answer it.

Six Fat Pigs

Six fat pigs on a ship,

Dip,

   Dip,

      Dip for fish.

A fish for duck, and one for cat,

And the pigs can have their wish.

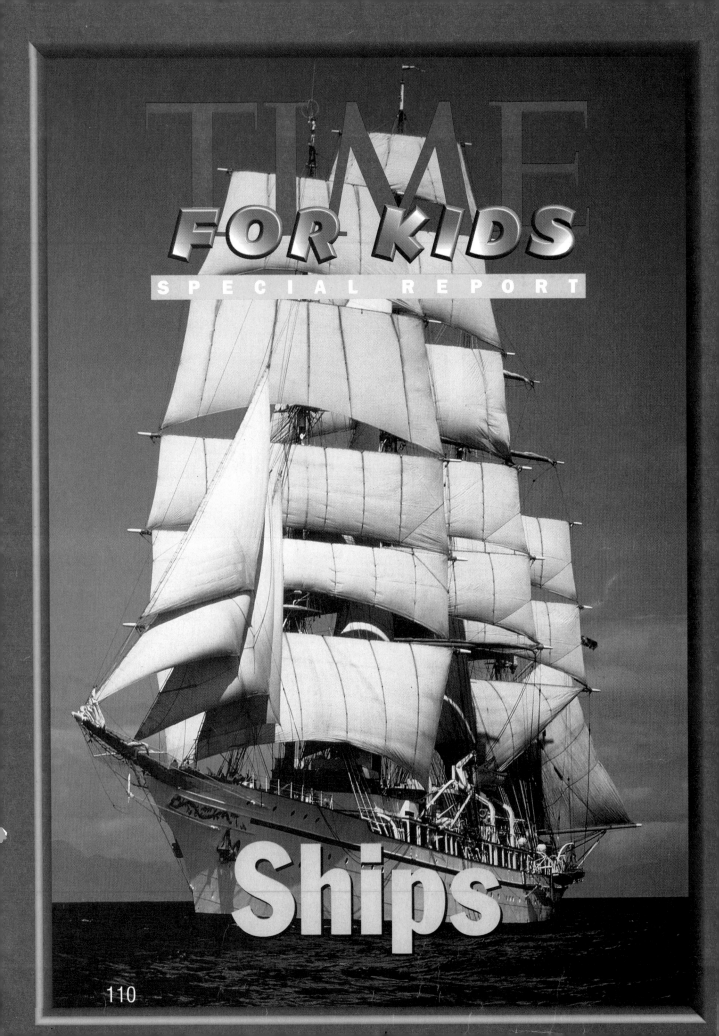

TIME
FOR KIDS
SPECIAL REPORT

Ships

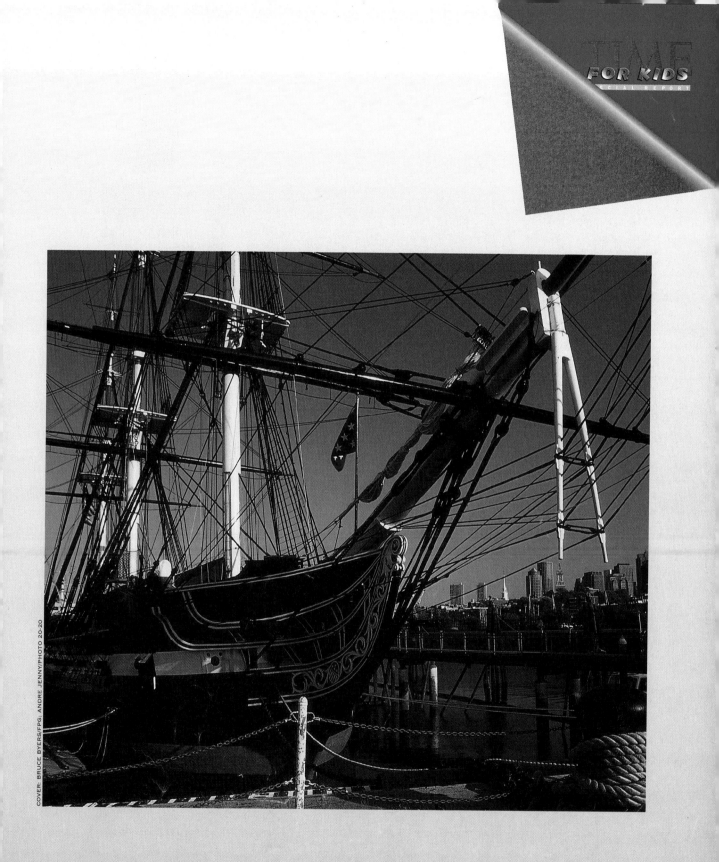

Look at the big ship.

It has sails.

This one is a steam ship.

Look at this ship.

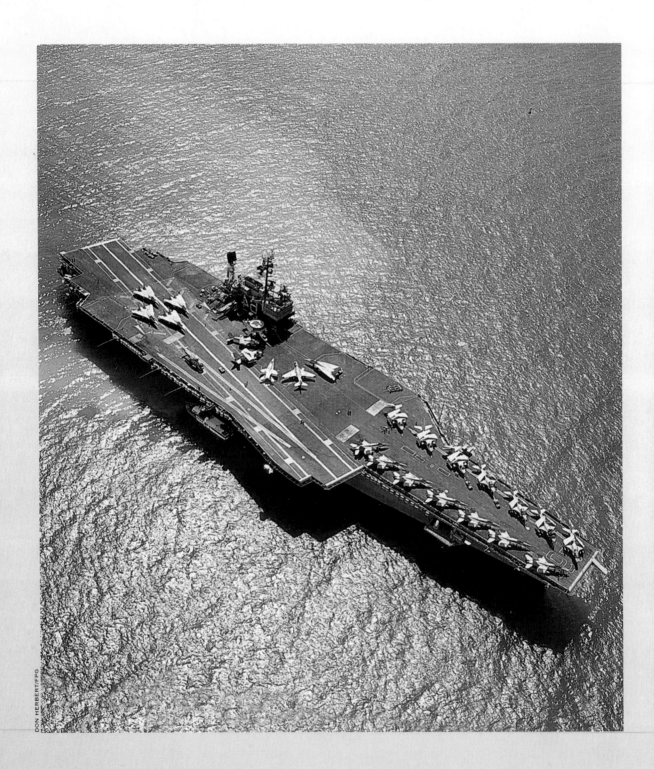

It is a Navy ship.

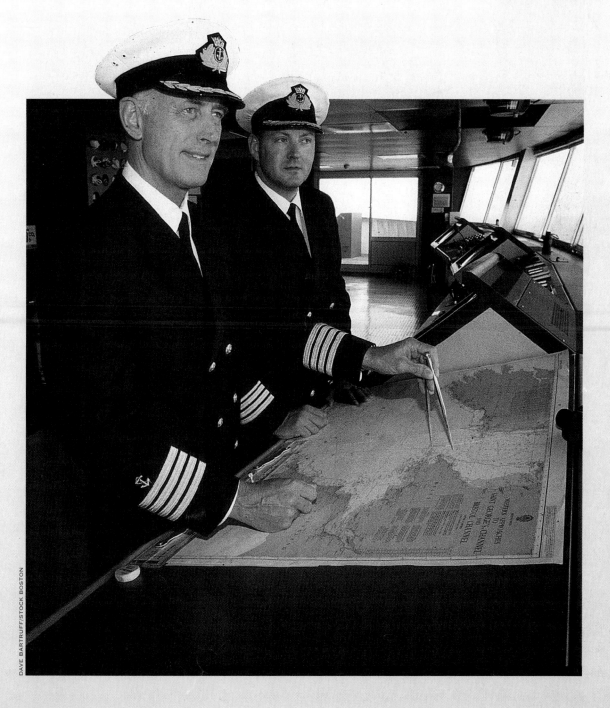

What ship is that?

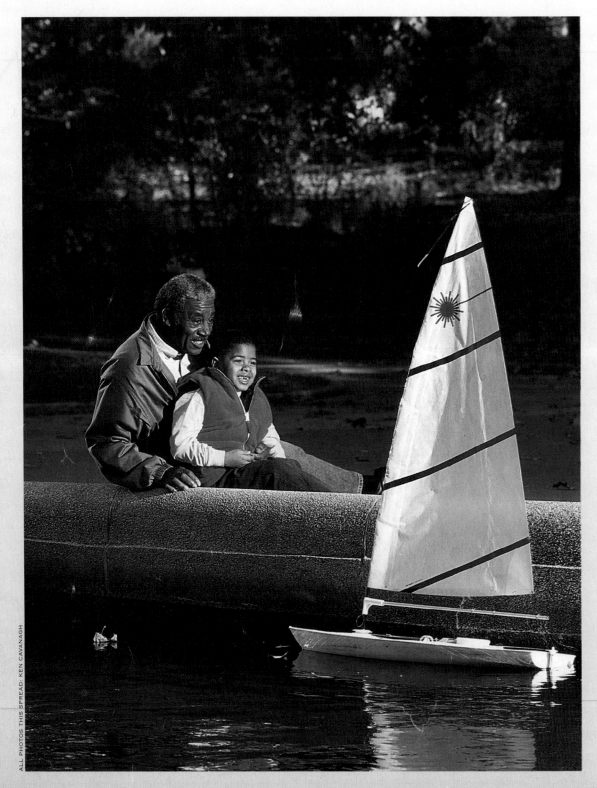

A story from the editors of *TIME FOR KIDS*.

This one is my ship!

Story Questions & Activities

1 What did the first ship have?

2 What helps a big ship move?

3 When is it better to use a ship than a truck?

4 Name ships you read about.

5 What other story in this unit shows a way of getting places?

Write a Log

Pretend you are on a ship.
Write about what happens.

Monday: October 4, 2002
We had to fix a sail.

Make a Raft

Use heavy cardboard.

Draw a raft shape on it.

Cut out the raft.

Make a notch in the back.

Put a bit of soap in the notch.

See if the raft floats in water.

Find Out More

Find out one new thing about ships.

Write a sentence.

Draw a picture and name your ship.

STUDY SKILLS

Parts of a Magazine

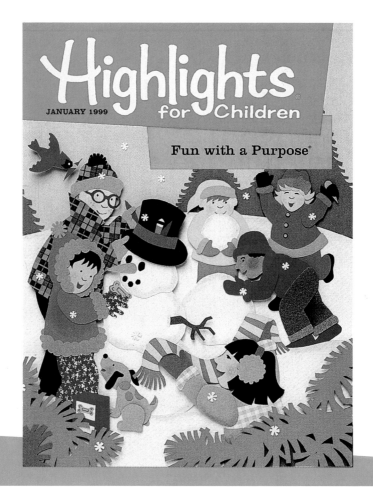

Look at the Magazine Cover

1 What is the name of the magazine?

2 What pictures are on the cover?

Get Up

Get up Sun.

It is day.

Rise up in the sky.

Shine all day.

Shine on the ships on the sea.

Shine on the shells on the beach.

Shine on you.

Shine on me.

Look for the answer that fits the story.

In this story,

the sun shines on —

○ the hills

○ the ships

A Year Later

by Mary Ann Hoberman

Last summer I couldn't swim at all;

I couldn't even float;

I had to use a rubber tube

Or hang on to a boat;

I had to sit on shore

While everybody swam;

But now it's this summer

And I can!

123

Glossary

This glossary can help you to find out the meanings of words in this book that you may not know.

The words are listed in alphabetical order. There is a picture and a simple sentence for each word. You can use the picture and sentence to help you understand the meaning of each word.

Sample Entry

Main Entry **Sample Sentence**

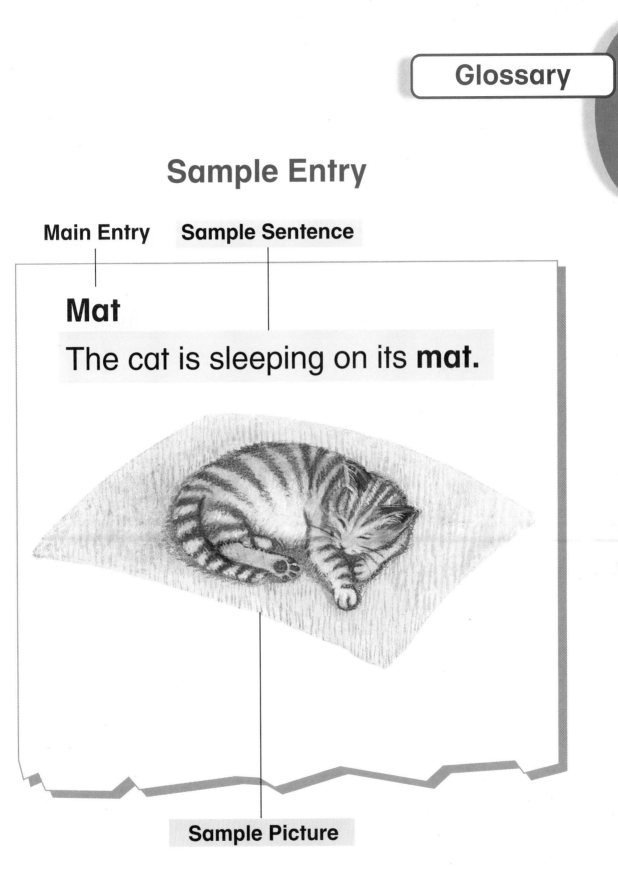

Mat

The cat is sleeping on its **mat.**

Sample Picture

Bat

Jim hits the ball with a **bat.**

Big

Our beach ball is **big.**

Cap

Zack wears his team's **cap.**

Cow

A **cow** is a farm animal that gives milk.

Dig

Nick uses a shovel to **dig.**

Fish

Fish live in the water.

Hat

Farmer Tad is wearing a **hat** on his head.

Hug

Cal gets a **hug** from Mom.

Map

A **map** shows where places are.

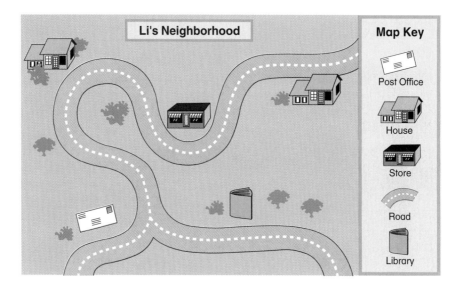

Mat

The cat is sleeping on its **mat.**

Path

A clear **path** makes it easier to get into your home.

Sails

The **sails** help the boats move.

Ship

A **ship** is a big boat.

Steam

The **steam** is coming out of the ship's stack.

Van

We ride a **van** to school.

Wig

A **wig** can be fun to wear.

ACKNOWLEDGMENTS

The publisher gratefully acknowledges permission to reprint the following copyrighted material:

"The Tickle Rhyme" by Ian Serraillier. Reprinted by permission.

"A Year Later" from THE LLAMA WHO HAD NO PAJAMA: 100 FAVORITE POEMS. Copyright 1959 and renewed 1987 by Mary Ann Hoberman. Reprinted by permission of Harcourt, Inc.

Illustration

Jack Graham, 6–7; Mircea Catusanu, 8–9; Kathi Ember, 10–27, 28tl; Daniel Del Valle, 28br, 29tr, 53tr, 79cr, 105; Ken Bowser, 31, 107; Michele Noiset, 32–33; Luisa D'Augusta, 34–51, 52 tl; Doug Roy, 52, 106; Bernard Adnet, 55 br, 121br; Mas Miyamoto, 55tr, 121tr; Darcia Labrosse, 56–57; Barbara Reid, 58–78; Eldon Doty, 81; Don Sullivan, 82–83; Peggy Tagel, 84–103; Jennifer Rarey, 108–9; Cecily Lang, 122–3; Felipe Galindo, 126, 128; Holly Jones, 127, 130 Peter Fasolino, 129, 133.

Photography

10: b. Courtesy of H.K Portfolio Inc.; t. courtesy of Ann Morris. 29: Photodisc. 34: b. Courtesy of Luisa D'Augusta; t. courtesy of Judi Barrett. 53: Photodisc; Photodisc; Photodisc. 58: b. Noodle Studio/(c) Ian Crysler '97; t. Diva Productions, Inc./Diva Productions, Inc.. 84: b. Courtesy HK Portfolio; t.l. Ellen Warner; Index Stock Photography/; The Stock Market. 85: The Stock Market/Gary Landsman. 95: The Stock Market. 97: Photo Researchers, Inc./National Audubon Society. 98: FPG International/Larry West/FPG International. 101: The Stock Market/; The Stock Market/; Tony Stone Images/Kathi Lamm. 103: FPG International/American Images; FPG International/Larry West; 126: . 127: b. Tony Stone Images/Renee Lynn. 128: . 129: Tony Stone Images. 131: b. The Stock Market/Jim Brown. t. Tony Stone Images/Gay Bumgarner; 132: The Stock Market/Ray Soto. b. Tony Stone Images/(c) Nancy Simmerman; 133: Douglas Pebbles.